Starting and Marksmanship

Richard Float

Amateur Athletic Association

The Crowood Press

First published in 1987 by
The Crowood Press
Ramsbury, Marlborough
Wiltshire SN8 2HE

British Library Cataloguing in Publication Data

Float, Richard
Starting and marksmanship.
1.   Track-athletics—Rules
I. Title
796.4'26   GV1060. 67

ISBN 1-85223-022-3

Picture Credits
Figs 1, 5, 6, 9, 10, 11, 12 and 13 are by
Associated Sports Photography.

Typeset by Lee Typesetting, Warminster
Printed in Great Britain

Contents

Acknowledgements   4

Preface   5

1 The Duties and Responsibilities of Starters and Marksmen   7

2 Pre-meeting Preparations by the Starting Team   9

3 The Marksmen   11

4 The Qualities of an Ideal Starter   17

5 The Personal Equipment of the Starter   19

6 Starting Procedure and Technique   23

7 Indoor Athletics   44

8 Major Championships and International Meetings   47

9 Conclusion   54

Appendices   55

Acknowledgements

The booklet *The Technique of Starting*, written by John W. Aspland, first appeared in the AAA series of official publications in 1963. The procedures which were set out so comprehensively over twenty years ago have altered very little; the need for this new booklet arises almost entirely from factors such as changes in the Rules of Competition. As the author of this new booklet I must therefore record that athletics in this country continues to remain indebted to John Aspland for his long-standing contribution to the art of Starting and Marksmanship.

I am also pleased to have the opportunity of thanking the following for their assistance: Miss Linda Duncan, who undertook the unenviable task of typing the manuscript; George Herringshaw (Associated Sports Photography) who provided all the photographs, with the exception of the shots of the false start apparatus for which I am indebted to Barry Craighead; Phil Tomkins and Roy West, two of my Chief Starter colleagues, and Alan Tomkins, all of whom read and commented most constructively upon my drafts.

It is only proper that I should also acknowledge here the help and friendship that I have enjoyed over the last twenty or so years from technical officials of all disciplines. It is obviously impossible to mention by name all those with whom I have been involved since I first took up Starting, but I trust that nobody will take it amiss if I do acknowledge an especial debt to Dan Davies, Alan Tomkins, Phil Tomkins and A.H. 'Dickie' Wilmot. Without their assistance and encouragement I would not have become a Chief Starter and thus reached the position where I have been invited to write this booklet.

Richard Float
March 1987

Preface

The Combined Officials' Committee of the AAA and WAAA has a well-established system of testing and grading technical officials. Details of the operation of this system can be found in the current AAA and WAAA Handbooks. The aim of this booklet is to provide guidance on the correct way to officiate for anyone who wants to act as a Starter or Marksman at the grass-root levels of club or school athletics. Equally, it is designed to assist candidates for the AAA and WAAA Test because it is hoped that those who become involved in officiating at a club or school will want to take the Combined Officials' Examination and seek graded status.

Promotion through the grades establishes that an individual is regarded as competent to officiate first at county and then, in turn, at area, national and international levels of competition. In addition, it is a requirement that the officials in charge of an event are graded if an athlete's performance is to be put forward as a record. Starters and Marksmen are therefore urged to take the written Test, which is not onerous provided the candidate has studied the rules and relevant procedures. It is desirable, although not essential, for a candidate to have had some practical experience of starting, even if this is only at a very informal level with groups of athletes at training sessions.

The syllabus for the Starters' and Marksmen's Tests covers the Rules of Competition and also requires a knowledge of the accepted methods of applying these rules; put simply, while a sound knowledge of the rules is obviously fundamental and can be readily acquired by rote-learning methods, the Tests, particularly those for Starters, rightly place emphasis on candidates being able to show whether or not they are familiar with the accepted procedures for applying the rules. These common procedures, which are outlined in Chapters 1 to 6, greatly assist in the smooth running of any meeting and give athletes the assurance that all competitions will be conducted along broadly similar lines.

The booklet incorporates two further chapters, Chapter 7 on indoor athletics and Chapter 8 on procedures at major national and international meetings. The material contained in these two chapters is not part of the Test syllabus, but has been included for the sake of general interest. Indoor meetings are now an established and important part of the athletics calendar and, it is felt, merit separate comment. It is hoped that the section on major meetings will provide some insight into officiating at this level and may, perhaps, assist and encourage more officials to seek the necessary experience to enable them to earn promotion to the senior grades.

It should be noted that unlike Timekeepers, Track Judges and Field Judges, there is no Advanced Examination for Starters and Marksmen seeking promotion to Grade I. Promotion to this level can only be achieved if senior Starters are satisfied that an individual has demonstrated over a period that he or she is worthy of promotion by the quality of his or her performance at meetings. Promotion to Chief Starter is dependent on these practical skills, but there must also be an ability to lead a team of officials. For this reason appointment to the grade of Chief cannot be won by length of service alone; these officials are not just better-than-average Grade I Starters but are also capable team leaders.

Note This booklet is based on the Rules of Competition currently in force. These can be found in the AAA Handbook 1986-7 edition, the WAAA Handbook 1985 edition (revised) and, where appropriate, the International Amateur Athletic Association (IAAF) Handbook 1985-6 edition. (It is envisaged that a joint rulebook will be introduced from 1 April 1987 which will serve both Men's and Women's Associations.)

1

The Duties and Responsibilities of Starters and Marksmen

THE STARTER

1. Controls absolutely all matters relating to the start. It should be noted that his decision is final and cannot be overruled by the Referee.
2. Ensures a good, fair start for all competitors. If a competitor is responsible for a false start the Starter must warn or disqualify him in accordance with the Rules of Competition.
3. Assists in keeping the meeting to timetable.

THE MARKSMAN

1. Acts under the overall direction of the Starter, although there are usually three Marksmen of whom one is designated Chief Marksman to lead the team.
2. Checks that competitors are present, correctly attired and wearing numbers in accordance with the programme.
3. Arranges the draw for stations and then places competitors in their correct lanes.
4. Checks for infringements while athletes are on their marks.

At major meetings, that is at area level and above, Start Recallers are appointed from within the team of Starters. If in the opinion of a Start Recaller a start was not fair, and the Starter does not recall the competitors with a second shot, the Start Recaller will do so by firing his gun. In practice the first opportunity to recall rests with the Starter who has the sole responsibility after a recall of deciding whether a warning, or disqualification, should be enforced.

For smaller meetings at club level one Starter is adequate, but it is prudent to ensure that either a second Starter, or a Marksman who is equipped and capable of acting as a Starter, is available in case of unforeseen circumstances that at the last minute might prevent the appointed official from appearing. It is difficult to run a successful meeting without a Starter! Two, or preferably three, Marksmen should be appointed, of whom one should be designated Chief. These officials make up the typical starting team.

2
Pre-meeting Preparations by the Starting Team

All the officials in the starting team should arrive at the ground at least half an hour before the first track event is due. It is emphasised that half an hour is the *minimum* time: any Starter or Marksman who is not familiar with the layout of a particular track should take steps to arrive considerably earlier.

Upon arrival, the Starters and Marksmen should report to the Meeting Secretary and obtain a copy of the official programme. This should be carefully checked with any preliminary time-tables that have been issued and for any special rules or requirements of the meeting. It is also helpful if the Starter lets the Track Referee know that he has arrived and establishes who is the Chief Timekeeper and how this official will signal that his team is ready for each race, for example by waving a flag or raising a programme attached to a clipboard above his head. The use of a chequered flag is the most satisfactory method and is to be preferred. The Starter should then seek out the other members of his team if they have not already contacted him.

It is recommended that all the starting team should check the track markings before the meeting commences, particularly with reference to events such as the steeplechase where start and finish lines are not always in standardised positions.

The Starter should take the opportunity of deciding where he will position himself for the start of each distance: there may be problems with ground equipment, and sometimes the Starter may find that jumping pits and throwing arcs will interfere with his normal positioning. These routine checks are especially important if there is a 4 × 400m relay event with a long echelon (first 500m in lanes) which requires a very large area to be free of equipment. It should also be established that there is sufficient space for athletes to be assembled near to, but clear of, the vicinity of each start.

9

If the track is provided with a rostrum and with a microphone to amplify the starting commands, the Starter should check this equipment. He should ensure that the microphone cables are long enough, that all the microphone points are working, and that the speaker volume is set correctly.

Finally, he should ensure that he is aware of the Timekeepers' position, and that they will be able to see him clearly at the points he has selected for starting races at the various distances.

In addition, the Marksmen should check, if necessary with the Clerk of the Course, that there is an adequate supply of starting blocks and relay batons.

These preliminaries will be completed quite quickly if the officials are familiar with the track, but may take a little while if the Starter or his colleagues are visiting a particular track for the first time. It is for this reason that it is again emphasised that arrival only half an hour beforehand is to be regarded as the absolute minimum.

This pre-meeting period is also a useful time for the Starter to brief his team, particularly if one or more of them is inexperienced or unknown to him. If there is more than one Starter, the one designated as Chief Starter for the meeting will indicate by means of a written list which races he will start and which races his colleague(s) will handle. Duties are usually allocated so that the start of the heats, any subsequent rounds, and the final of the same event are undertaken by the same Starter (*see* Appendix III).

When all these preliminaries have been completed, the Starter should leave the arena to change and to check personal equipment. He should re-enter the arena about fifteen minutes before the first track event is timed to commence.

3
The Marksmen

The Marksmen are a very important part of the starting team. The more efficiently they perform, the more smoothly a meeting will run, and the Starter will be able to concentrate on the task of starting without having to worry about other details.

The duties of Marksmen, even at major meetings, have usually been carried out by officials who have qualified as Starters. This arrangement continues, but in addition the Combined Officials' Committee has now established a grading system for those who wish to act only as Marksmen. This has been a major step in recognising the value of Marksmen, the importance of whose duties has, perhaps, been underrated in the past.

The skills of Marksmanship and Starting are not very similar, but the grading system requires Starters to be qualified in Marksmanship from the outset because the duties of these officials are complementary. Starters cannot progress through the grading system unless they show at each level that they are competent Marksmen as well as competent Starters. This point is worth emphasising for those who aspire to progress as Starters.

A Marksman requires the following equipment:

1.   A supply of spare competitors' numbers, to replace those lost or mutilated, together with plenty of safety pins.
2.   A means of drawing for lanes.
3.   A clipboard for the meeting programme, with a transparent plastic cover or bag that fits over it so that the user can write on a dry surface when it is raining.
4.   A Chinagraph pencil and a thick marker pen. The former is for writing, while the latter is useful to produce makeshift competitors' numbers when spares are not available.
5.   A spike gauge, because at all-weather tracks there is a restriction on the length of spike permitted.
6.   A reliable watch to assist in keeping the meeting running to

time.
7.   Waterproof clothing and footwear.

The pre-meeting preliminaries have already been dealt with in Chapter 2. It is now necessary to outline the sequence of duties which the team of Marksmen perform prior to the start of each race at the direction of the Chief Marksman.

1.   Ten minutes or so before the event is due to start the names and numbers of all the competitors must be called out at the appropriate starting point to establish who is present and checked against the programme. This procedure is known as *call-up*. The Rules prohibit any athlete from receiving assistance during a race and from being accompanied on the mark. Any friend, coach or helper straying into the arena at the call-up stage must be asked to leave immediately.
2.   If heats with competitors' stations have been pre-drawn by Seeders, the athletes should be told to which heat and lane they have been allotted. It should be noted that only the Track Referee has the power to rearrange such a draw. If, however, the event has not been pre-drawn, the Marksmen must arrange the draw, usually by means of numbered draw cards or sticks. Lane 1 is always on the left when facing in the direction of the race.
3.   At the same time, the opportunity must be taken to check that the clothing and shoes of all the competitors comply with the Rules, including those relating to advertising, and that each athlete is wearing the correct number. It is important that numbers are pinned firmly to the athletes' vests. The AAA and WAAA Rules require that numbers are not torn, defaced or folded, but 'worn as issued'.
4.   If photo finish is in use, self-adhesive leg numbers will have to be issued.
5.   If the race is a heat the athletes must be informed of the qualifying conditions for the next round.
6.   Starting blocks may be used in races up to and including 400m. The Marksmen must check that when in position on the track the blocks do not overlap the starting line or project beyond the lane in question. If any competitor wishes to use personal starting blocks, the construction of which must comply

with the Rules, the approval of the Starter must be sought.

7.   If the event is an 800m race from an echelon start, or a 4 × 400m relay, the athletes should be advised of the point at which they may break from their lanes and the colour of the line on the track which marks this point.

8.   The Starter should be advised of the number of heats and how many competitors there will be in each heat.

9.   About three minutes before the event is due, the athletes must be told to remove their track suits and must then be marshalled on the assembly line, three metres behind the start line, each athlete in the correct lane.

10.   After a quick visual check that all is in order and that, for example, all competitors' numbers are still firmly in position, the Chief Marksman should give a signal to the Starter that the athletes are ready by raising his clipboard above his head. The Starter will then establish that the Timekeepers are ready by means of a whistle and, on receiving the Chief Timekeeper's signal, prepare to issue his first command: 'On your marks'.

Although from this point on the Starter assumes full control of the athletes, the duties of the Marksmen have not ended; continuing co-operation with the Starter is needed to ensure that there are no infringements. From Figs 2 to 4 it will be seen that:

11.   On straight sprint starts the Chief Marksman should take up a position *opposite* the Starter, from which he can watch along the starting line for hand faults. It should be noted that athletes using a crouch start must have *both* hands in contact with the ground. The other Marksmen should take positions to the rear, from which they can observe unobtrusively and not block the view of Lane Umpires. It should not be necessary for Marksmen to walk in front of or between athletes on their marks, as this will only serve to unsettle them (*see* Fig 2).

12.   On echelon starts, each Marksman should watch two or three athletes for hand faults, moving forward and checking them from the outside (*see* Figs 3 and 4). The Chief Marksman must always be responsible for the two or three athletes in the outer lanes so that when he has completed his check he can face the Starter, looking back down the entire field.

Fig 1   Athletes getting to their marks for a 100m sprint. The two Marksmen have not yet completed their checks, but will walk to the opposite sides of the straight as soon as the athletes have settled (see also Fig 2).

At this stage no signal should be given unless there is an infringement, in which case the Marksman concerned must step forward and raise his clipboard above his head so that the Starter can see that all is not well. The Marksman must tell the athlete concerned what is wrong, leaving the Starter to order the athletes to stand up. When each Marksman is satisfied after conducting his checks, he should step back a few paces to the edge of the track and remain motionless. When all movement has ceased, the Starter will give the command 'Set' and, if satisfied that the athletes are steady, will fire his gun.

If there is a false start, the Starter will decide and announce who is responsible. The Chief Marksman must then convey the warning to the offending athlete(s) except in the case of echelon starts where, to save time, the nearest Marksman to the offender should administer the warning. It is recommended that any athlete who is warned should be asked to raise his hand to acknowledge the warning, and if lane marker boxes are available a red light or flag should be displayed. The Marksmen must also note the number of the offending athlete(s) so that whenever more than one false start occurs there is a clear record of the warnings previously given in case any athlete offends a second time. After a false start the competitors should be placed once more on the assembly line.

For races above 400m the command 'Set' is omitted and athletes do not use a crouch start, but the procedures prior to each start are the same as outlined above. For 800m races using an echelon start the Marksmen must conduct their checks in similar fashion to a 400m race, but for 800m races run off a curved starting line, and for longer distance events, a slightly different procedure is adopted. The Chief Marksman should stand at the opposite end of the starting line to the Starter and ensure that none of the competitors encroaches on to it. The other Marksmen should stand behind the field. Where the starting line is on a bend the athletes should not be placed in the lane next to the kerb, because anyone in this position is liable to be shut out by the rest of the field (*see* Figs 7 and 8). After the command 'On your marks', and when all the competitors are motionless at the starting line, the Starter will fire the gun. It is therefore important for a Marksman to be sure to signal the Starter before attempting to speak to an athlete.

As soon as a race gets under way satisfactorily, there is no time to spectate or to gossip with fellow officials. The Marksmen should move on to the next heat or event, but must first ensure that the false start indicators are cancelled and that the track is clear by removing starting blocks and other personal items that may have been inadvertently left lying around.

The duties of the Marksmen are generally straightforward but are often undertaken under pressure, particularly when there is a large number of competitors who must be kept quiet and out of line of the Starter's vision while races are being started. Three Marksmen are usually required, but on an eight lane track, or where there are large fields, a fourth is desirable.

Besides the specific tasks listed above, it has previously been noted that the Chief Marksman is responsible for allocating duties to his team. He should indicate who should be responsible for call-up, who should check clothing, who should check numbers, and so on. It is customary to rotate these duties amongst the team so that each Marksman can take a turn at each job. Clear written instructions are essential so that everybody is fully aware of what is expected of them (*see* Appendix IV). It is, however, recommended that the Chief Marksman should be responsible throughout the meeting for one very important function: he should signal to the Starter when all is ready prior to the start of each race. If the number of Marksmen in relation to the size of the meeting permits, it is best that the Chief Marksman does not undertake call-up and preliminary checks, but adopts the role of overseeing the others in his team, stepping in to assist where problems arise or a hold-up seems likely to develop.

The important point is that to perform satisfactorily Marksmen need to be well-organised by their Chief; this will enable them to carry out their duties in an efficient but quiet fashion. They must be patient but firm, thereby gaining the co-operation of the athletes. Although a clear, strong and authoritative voice is often necessary, a bullying manner must be avoided at all costs.

4

The Qualities of an
Ideal Starter

It is not hard to imagine the contrast between starting races in informal surroundings, such as the typical club meeting, and starting a field of eight highly-strung, temperamental and very competitive athletes in a short sprint at an international competition in front of a packed stadium. The actual starting technique in both cases will have much in common, but its application in these very different circumstances will not necessarily be as easy as it might seem, quite apart from the additional problem created by the pressures and tensions of top level track and field athletics.

In order to perform well the Starter first needs a sound basic knowledge of the rules, which can normally be acquired quite quickly. He will also need a great deal of practice at starting races for which there is no short cut and which will require a considerable degree of dedication to the sport. Accordingly, a Starter should seize every opportunity to widen his experience, particularly if this can involve working at meetings with senior officials who will be able to offer advice and guidance.

In both the competitive situations described above, the decisions of the Starter are final. It is thus absolutely essential that the Starter is completely up to date in his knowledge of the Rules and knows how to interpret them quickly, correctly and with confidence. It must never be forgotten that races can be decided by margins of less than a hundredth of a second (the equivalent of ten centimetres or thereabouts at top level sprinting speeds) and there is therefore no room for even the tiniest error by this official at the start.

For such an important role the Starter must be physically fit with good eyesight, and must be mentally alert. The ideal Starter should couple these qualities with a number of other attributes, although a glance at the list will rapidly reveal that the description is indeed more likely to be of an ideal than of reality! These attributes are:

1.   Quick reactions – in order to respond immediately to any infringement or problem. The Starter has to make difficult decisions on his own, quickly, but without panic.

2.   Good command – a Starter must be firmly in charge. The athletes will respond to this in a positive way, trusting the ability of the Starter to ensure that everyone has a fair start. This extremely desirable sense of rapport can be obtained by a quiet, courteous and authoritative manner, and not by being aggressive or overbearing.

3.   A clear speaking voice – it will greatly enhance the efficiency of his command if the Starter conveys his decisions with clarity. 'Clear speaking' must not, however, be confused with shouting in a parade-ground manner which is highly undesirable.

4.   Self-confidence – this is essential because weakness or indecision will rapidly erode any rapport between Starter and athletes.

5.   Determination and patience – these are very necessary qualities if difficult situations are to be overcome.

6.   Impartial judgement – the Starter's decisions must be given without fear or favour, and may sometimes adversely affect a fellow club member or, at international level, a fellow countryman.

The question is often asked if it is helpful for Starters to have had competitive experience as sprinters, since the most common problems that they will encounter are with sprint starts. First-hand experience as a sprinter can undoubtedly be most useful, and sprinters possess quick reactions which are also required. It would be beneficial if more ex-sprinters did take an interest in officiating as Starters, provided that they have a fair share of the other qualities outlined above.

5

The Personal Equipment
of the Starter

Starters are required to wear a red cap and red blazer in order that they can be seen easily by the Timekeepers. Nowadays white trousers and white shoes are worn at major meetings, but these are not essential at club level. What is important at all times is a smart appearance; the Starter in his red blazer is conspicuous and a good appearance will help to project an air of competence and efficiency, whereas an untidy, slovenly turn-out will have the opposite effect.

The other basic items of personal equipment are:

1.   Two revolvers, one for starting and one for recalling, both with open-ended barrels.
2.   A plentiful supply of blank ammunition containing a black powder charge. Modern explosives are unsuitable because they do not give the necessary flash or smoke of traditional gunpowder.
3.   A whistle, in order to check prior to the start of each race that the Timekeepers are ready. The whistle is best kept in the outer breast pocket of the jacket and can be secured neatly by a white lanyard around the neck.
4.   Waterproof clothing. An anorak and trousers are the most common rainwear with red again the desirable colour, although many Starters now have white waterproof trousers. Waterproof shoes or overshoes (galoshes) are useful in wet weather.
5.   A reliable watch, because it is one of the responsibilities of the Starter to keep the meeting to timetable.
6.   A screwdriver, which can be invaluable in the rare but potentially embarrassing occurrence of mechanical problems with a gun.
7.   A current Firearm Certificate.

Many Starters like to have with them a clipboard for the meeting programme, and it is also sensible to take along lane-drawing equipment, spare safety pins and spare competitors' numbers in case these prove to be in short supply. A copy of the current Rules of Competition is also essential, although the competent official will only use it as evidence to support his decisions at any discussion after the meeting and will not otherwise need to refer to it.

A little more needs to be said about the most fundamental of all these items, namely the Starter's guns. First, it must be made clear that any firearm is potentially dangerous and must be treated with care at all times. Many people believe that blank cartridges are harmless, but this is not true. The wads at the end of the cartridges can cause injury at close quarters, and powder burns and blast injuries can also be sustained, even from guns with blocked barrels. The following common-sense rules must be observed:

1. Do not point a gun at anybody, even in fun.
2. Do not cock the starting gun until it is necessary.
3. Do not hold a gun close to your own face.
4. Ensure that guns are not left lying around during the course of a meeting where they could be interfered with by other people. (Guns have an unfailing fascination for young athletes!)
5. Do not allow your guns to be borrowed or examined.
6. Do not leave guns loaded after use.
7. Do not tamper with cartridges.

Closely allied to these safety measures, and to ensure reliability, it is strongly recommended that guns are cleaned and checked without fail after every meeting because there is nothing more unnerving for a Starter and for the athletes than a gun misfiring. The residues of black powder cartridges can clog the mechanism if allowed to accumulate. They are also highly corrosive and must be removed by flushing the barrel and chambers with boiling water, followed by the use of a bronze brush with a proprietary cleaner. The weapon should then be dried with lint-free cloth and lightly oiled. It is also advisable to have guns serviced from time to time by a competent gunsmith.

It is wise for Starters to take out third party insurance cover so that they are fully protected in respect of legal liability if involved in an accident with their guns. Most insurance companies are willing to extend the normal Householder's Policy to cover this eventuality and will usually do so at no extra charge.

The selection of guns is an important matter. The best type, and the one commonly in use by senior Starters, is the .455 inch revolver. Unfortunately, this calibre and its ammunition are increasingly hard to obtain, but it is well worth making the effort to do so because both the volume of the report and the flash and smoke are much superior to those of smaller calibre weapons. The loudness of the report is particularly important in long echelon starts, where the athletes in the outer lanes are well away from the Starter, while plenty of flash and smoke are vital for hand-timing.

A pair of .38 inch calibre revolvers is the best alternative. This size of gun is more easily obtained and there are no problems with the supply of ammunition, which is considerably cheaper. Many of these guns will also accept 9mm cartridges. Smaller calibres than this, for example .32 inch and .22 inch, are considered to give inadequate signals, especially for accurate hand-timing purposes, and their use is not recommended.

Whichever of the two preferred calibres is chosen, it is important that the guns are a matched pair so that the recall shot is as distinct as the starting one. A reasonably light trigger action is desirable. The guns should have open-ended barrels because this concentrates the flash and smoke at the muzzle, thereby giving the best possible signal for hand-timing. In addition, when an electric timing device is in use, a transducer, which activates the timing system, is often attached to the Starter's gun; this will not be possible if the weapon has gas vent holes in the side of a blocked barrel.

Any would-be Starter who is about to purchase a pair of guns is urged very strongly to seek advice by contacting an experienced Starter through the local County or District Secretary. He can then be directed to a good gunsmith to find out what is available and the price.

Following this it will be necessary to obtain an application form for a Firearm Certificate from the Chief Constable of the police force of the area in which the Starter resides. The police will require to be satisfied that the guns will be kept in a secure place, such as a safe or a securely-fixed lockable strong box. If difficulties are encountered in obtaining the Certificate, particularly with regard to the request for open-barrelled guns, the assistance of the local County, District or Area Secretary should be sought in support of the application. When the Firearm Certificate has been obtained, the Starter will be able to proceed with the purchase of the guns he has selected. He must, however, note carefully and observe the conditions under which the Certificate is granted, particularly the requirement that it must be carried by him wherever the guns are taken.

6
Starting Procedure and Technique

It has been explained how the Marksmen prepare athletes for a race, thus enabling the Starter to concentrate on his own responsibilities and to remain aloof from these preliminaries until he takes over and commences the actual starting procedure. Nevertheless, it must be emphasised that the Starter does have overall control of the starting team and he must not hesitate to exert his authority if he finds that Marksmen are failing in their duty because of, for example, inexperience. In these cases he should convey his requirements firmly but quietly to the Chief Marksman in order to ensure that matters are put right immediately.

POSITIONING FOR THE START

In Chapter 2 it was noted that before the meeting commences the Starter must check items such as the amplification equipment and rostrum, and the best position to take up at the start for each distance. In selecting the best position the Starter must satisfy four main requirements:

1. He must see all the athletes clearly.
2. He must be audible to the athletes.
3. He must be seen clearly by the Timekeepers.
4. The ground around must be free of clutter and obstructions.

To meet the first of these requirements the Starter must stand well back so that he sees the whole field evenly. Obviously, the things seen most clearly are those on which the eyes are focused, while the things on the fringe of this focal area are seen less clearly. By positioning himself at least 20m and probably closer

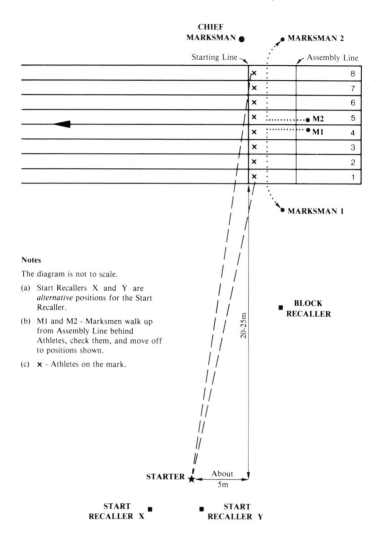

Fig 2 Positions at the start of a sprint race on the straight.

to 25m from the nearest athlete, the Starter will obtain the required even view of all the athletes. If he stands closer, he is likely to have a poorer view either of those nearest to him or those furthest from him, because the angle of vision will be too wide and he will not be able to focus on the whole field simultaneously. In turn, this may mean that the Starter is tempted to move his eyes or, even worse, his head in order to check on the athletes who are on the fringe of his line of sight. Such movement can prove fatal to concentration at a critical moment.

This principle of a narrow angle of vision holds good for both straight line and echelon starts. The position described above and shown in Figs 2 to 4 enables the Starter to line up the heads, arms and hands of the athletes on their marks within the desired narrow angle of vision, thereby giving a clear and even view of all the competitors. It is important to note that although an athlete using a crouch start makes a small initial movement of the back foot as the drive from the starting blocks begins, it is the hands which first break contact with the ground and which must be watched carefully.

The second requirement is that the Starter's commands are heard clearly by all the athletes. For straight line starts and 200m echelon races a clear speaking voice should be used and should generally be adequate even in the absence of amplification equipment. It is essential that commands are not bawled and that the tone adopted is calm but clear. Failure to observe this cardinal rule will invariably make nervous athletes more jumpy and increase the likelihood of false starts.

If there is no amplification equipment for the longer echelon of 400m, it is inevitable that the Starter will have to raise his voice considerably in order to be heard in the outside lanes. Fortunately, a fast get-away is not quite as essential at this distance and athletes are not as tense, so a raised voice tends not to cause jumpiness in the way that it would with a short sprint. Nevertheless, this does highlight the desirability of amplification equipment to enable all the athletes to hear simultaneously the Starter's commands given in normal speaking tones. The equipment is also useful in windy conditions. (*See* Appendix I for a description of 'do-it-yourself' amplification equipment which is very useful at tracks where this item is not part of the available

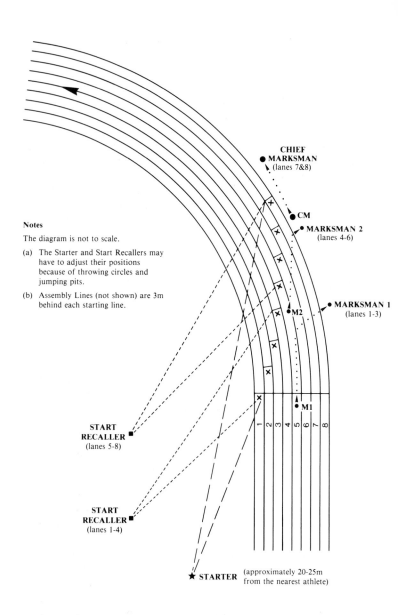

Notes

The diagram is not to scale.

(a) The Starter and Start Recallers may have to adjust their positions because of throwing circles and jumping pits.

(b) Assembly Lines (not shown) are 3m behind each starting line.

CHIEF MARKSMAN (lanes 7&8)

● **CM**

● **MARKSMAN 2** (lanes 4-6)

● **MARKSMAN 1** (lanes 1-3)

● **M2**

● **M1**

START RECALLER (lanes 5-8)

START RECALLER (lanes 1-4)

★ **STARTER** (approximately 20-25m from the nearest athlete)

Fig 3   Positions at the start of a 200m race.

26

equipment.)

Thirdly, it is important that the Timekeepers can easily locate the Starter and, having done so, can see the flash and smoke from his gun. It is also important that the Starter can see the Chief Timekeeper from whom he gets the signal that the officials at the finish are ready to time and judge the race. There are frequent occasions when a Starter will need to take great care in selecting his position so that items of ground equipment such as throwing cages and pole vault stands do not obstruct the Timekeepers' view. A rostrum is very helpful in raising the Starter above ground level (*see* Appendix II for a suitable design for this equipment) and a white cuff or half-sleeve worn on the gun arm can prove an additional help for the Timekeepers.

Finally, the ground around the Starter must be clear. This is necessary not only to eliminate distraction and ensure a clear view both for him and for the Timekeepers, but also for safety reasons.

STARTING PROCEDURE

The Starter should be ready in his chosen position about five minutes before an event is scheduled. In this way he can reassure himself that all is well and that there are no last minute problems.

Except in the case of very inexperienced youngsters, the Starter should not normally have cause to address athletes prior to a race but should remain detached from the proceedings. This will help to maintain the impartial attitude that is required. If, for some exceptional reason, it is necessary to speak to an athlete before the race, the competitor should be addressed by his number rather than name, thus placing emphasis on the fact that in a Starter's view competitors are numbered individuals rather than personalities.

One minute before the event is scheduled the Starter should mount the rostrum. As soon as he has received and acknowledged a signal from the Chief Marksman that the competitors are ready, he should blow a loud blast on his whistle to alert the Timekeepers and Judges. The use of a loud blast on the whistle should never be overlooked because, for example, the race is in the middle of a long series of heats, or because the Starter is standing near to the finish, as in a 400m race. Not only does the whistle alert the officials, but it also acts as a timely warning to everyone else, including the less observant Announcers, that a race is about to start, that the track must remain clear, and that the crowd should be hushed. Upon receiving the pre-arranged signal from the Chief Timekeeper that the officials at the finish are prepared, the Starter should make ready to get the race under way.

Next, the Starter should turn on the amplification equipment. This should not be done until after the officials at the finish have been whistled-up, because a blast on the whistle coming through the loudspeakers near to the competitors can be quite startling at a time when they are trying to calm their nerves and concentrate on the starting procedure. It is, however, wise to tap the microphone lightly each time after turning it on in order to establish that the system is still working correctly.

The Starter should then cock the starting gun. Cocking a gun minimises the amount of trigger pressure needed to fire it, thereby giving a virtually instantaneous response when the trigger is squeezed. The recall gun should not be cocked for two reasons: firstly, it may go off inadvertently when the Starter is getting down from the rostrum after a successful start; secondly, there must be a measured pause between the firing of the starting gun and any recall shot in order to avoid the possibility of the two reports merging into one.

The Starter should check that all athletes are still correctly assembled and that there has been no belated hitch, such as the Marksman noticing and having to secure a loose number. This check is important because a command issued before all is ready creates dither among the athletes. Uncertainty, with a sense of loss of control, is the very opposite of what is required. If all is well, and assuming for the moment that a sprint race is involved, the Starter will then issue the first starting command, 'On your marks' in a clear, precise voice, without either hurrying his words or drawling.

The athletes should be given adequate time to get down and settle into their crouch start positions, and while they are doing so the Starter should take the opportunity to make any minor adjustment in his own position, although he must continue to watch all the competitors carefully. If a Marksman signals that there is an infringement, usually a competitor encroaching on the starting line, or if the runners do not settle within a reasonable time, the command 'Stand up' must be given and the athletes must be reassembled. A brief word to the athlete or athletes responsible is advisable; this should be given clearly and courteously, not as a reprimand or in a bullying fashion, and then the first command, 'On your marks', should be given again.

When the athletes appear to have settled after the order 'On your marks', the Starter must be satisfied that all movement has ceased before the second starting command is given. Athletes often rock from side to side before becoming still, and even more frequently the head is dropped or the shoulders move forward slightly as the athlete takes his final position on the mark.

When all movement has ceased the Starter should be comfortably poised, looking down the line of athletes. After a slight pause he should slowly and smoothly raise his starting gun high above his head, moving his arm in an arc to the side or rear out of the line of his sight. He should then, if all is still, issue the command 'Set', in the same clear, firm speaking voice, taking care to avoid the extremes of either a sharp or a drawling tone. Concentration on the athletes, which is vital once the command 'On your marks' has been given, is even more essential at this stage so that the Starter can react immediately to any infringement or other incident.

Athletes pivot their head and shoulders forward over their hands at the same time as their rear leg extends and raises their hips when coming into the 'Set' position, but there is often a slight settling back at the conclusion of the forward movement. The Starter must ensure that this settling movement has ceased and that all competitors are absolutely motionless in their 'Set' position. After a pause, to allow the athletes to build up to peak concentration, the gun should be fired by deliberately squeezing the trigger. Any jerking or snatching movement should be avoided, as this may result in the gun moving which is most disconcerting to the Timekeepers.

The Starter must watch very carefully until the athletes have left the starting line lest any of the athletes anticipate the starting gun, even by the smallest margin, or become unsettled at the moment that the trigger is squeezed. If this is not the case and the foregoing procedure has been adopted, the Starter should have the satisfaction of seeing a strong, even response to the starting gun and all the competitors leaving the line together in a good, fair start.

After every race the Starter should switch off the microphone and then remove both the microphone and rostrum from the track if, as is often the case in a 400m race, it has been necessary to position them in the home straight. He should then reload his starting gun and, if there has been a false start, his recall gun.

HOLDING TIME

This is the pause in sprint races between the command 'Set' and the gun being fired which is vital for both the athletes and the Starter.

Holding time enables the athletes to concentrate on reacting to the gun after they have moved into the 'Set' position. It also enables the Starter to ensure that all the competitors are absolutely motionless in the 'Set' position.

A holding time that is too short will encourage some athletes to believe that they can anticipate the gun. Other athletes will become nervous, perhaps feeling that they will be at a disadvantage because they may not have time to come into their 'Set' position and pause for concentration, but instead may get left at the start. By contrast, over-long holds will allow peak concentration to pass and excessive tension to develop. In both cases there will be a lack of confidence in the Starter which will show itself in unsteadiness and far too many false starts.

In recent years, and particularly since the excellent standard of starting at Munich in the 1972 Olympic Games, it has become the accepted practice for holding times to average about two-and-a-half seconds instead of the two seconds which used to be favoured. The theory behind this holding time is roughly as follows:

1. It takes a tenth of a second or even a little more for the

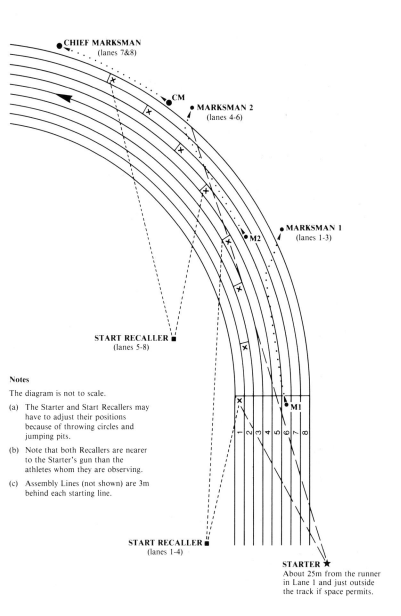

CHIEF MARKSMAN
(lanes 7&8)

CM

MARKSMAN 2
(lanes 4-6)

M2

MARKSMAN 1
(lanes 1-3)

START RECALLER ■
(lanes 5-8)

Notes

The diagram is not to scale.

(a) The Starter and Start Recallers may have to adjust their positions because of throwing circles and jumping pits.

(b) Note that both Recallers are nearer to the Starter's gun than the athletes whom they are observing.

(c) Assembly Lines (not shown) are 3m behind each starting line.

M1

START RECALLER ■
(lanes 1-4)

STARTER ★
About 25m from the runner in Lane 1 and just outside the track if space permits.

Fig 4   Positions at the start of a 400m race.

31

runner to hear and register the command 'Set'.

2. Between five- and seven-tenths of a second is then required for the runner to move into the 'Set' position.

3. Peak concentration then takes about another one-and-a-half seconds to develop.

These times are averages and will vary in different circumstances with the speed of movement and reaction of the athletes, but it is not hard to see that a holding time of, say, less than 1.8 seconds is almost certainly too fast while one of 3.0 seconds or more is likely to be too long.

It is the ability when under pressure to hold athletes in the 'Set' position, and thereby to ensure good, even starts, that is the real test of the Starter. Crowds often catcall and commentators are known to claim that there has been an over-long hold after a false start, although a check invariably reveals that the athletes have broken within, or even at less than, the holding range which has been suggested. In these circumstances the good Starter must steel himself not to compromise. If he shortens his holding time the athletes will try to anticipate and he will then fall into the danger of wanting to fire even faster to forestall breaks. He will thus lose control completely, putting his Starter colleagues at the meeting under unnecessary pressure when their turn comes, and causing confusion among even the best disciplined athletes.

A Starter can develop his sense of holding time by practice with a stop-watch but, while this can be useful, he must beware the effect that tension and crowd atmosphere can have on his judgement when starting races. There is no real substitute for race starting because personal judgement of the time interval is affected under the tension of a sprint start situation, and the pause after 'Set' in these circumstances can seem much longer than it actually is. For this reason a friend or colleague should be asked to check on holding time with a stop-watch under race conditions in order that the Starter can become accustomed to this factor and learn to judge the correct length of hold. After a false start occurs, particular attention should be paid to see if there is any shortening of the hold for the next attempt.

STARTING PROCEDURE FOR SPRINT RELAYS

The same procedure should be adopted for sprint relays, but the Starter should check before the Chief Timekeeper is whistled-up that each of the three take-over zones is ready by making in turn one, two, and then three whistle blasts. The Take-Over Judges should respond with white or red flags according to whether they are ready or not.

Fig 5   A good sprint start. Note how the hands of all the athletes have come away from the track almost in unison in response to the starting gun.

Fig 6   Another good start. All the athletes have responded powerfully and evenly to the gun. Note the Chief Marksman on the line opposite the Starter, one of the other Marksmen to the outside at the rear, and the Recaller next to the Starter.

STARTING PROCEDURE FOR RACES ABOVE 400M

The procedure incorporating the second starting command 'Set' is the one used for sprint races up to and including 400m.

For races above 400m the command 'Set' is omitted and athletes do not adopt a crouch start position. As soon as the athletes have responded to the command 'On your marks' by moving from the assembly line to the starting line, the Starter should raise his gun and, after a pause, fire when all the athletes are completely still. Although the concept of holding time does not apply, false starts can be quite common in middle distance events where athletes sometimes try to get rolling starts; it is important to watch the competitors carefully.

Notes

The diagram is not to scale.

(a) If there is insufficient room outside the track the Starter and Start Recaller will have to modify their positions. Alternatively they may prefer to come inside the track, in which case the Chief Marksman should go to the outside.

(b) The inner lane is not used by competitors for the start.

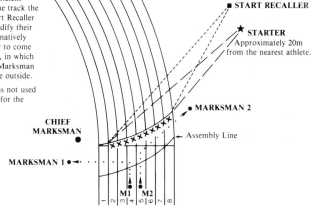

Fig 7   Positions at the start of an 800m race off a curved line.

Notes

The diagram is not to scale.

(a) The Starter may need to modify his position to take account of throwing circles and jumping pits.

(b) A Start Recaller is not considered necessary.

(c) The inner lane is not used by competitors for the start.

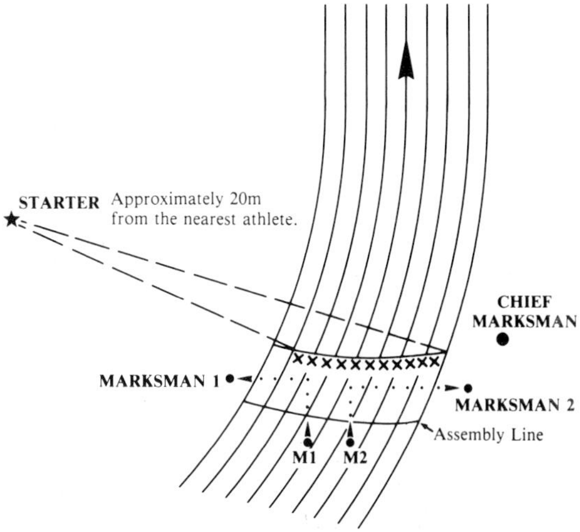

Fig 8   Positions at the start of a 1500m race.

35

As with crouch start races, it is essential that the gun is not held aloft too soon. If it is, the Timekeepers will be put under strain as they will have to concentrate for too long before the flash and smoke of the gun report are seen. Equally, the gun must not be raised and fired in one movement. The Timekeepers must be given an opportunity to focus their attention on the muzzle after the gun has been raised.

STAND-UP

This command is used for races at any distance if there is dissatisfaction with proceedings after 'On your marks' and before the gun is fired. Good Starters should never be shy of using it. Examples of its use are:

1. The athletes take too long to settle.
2. A Marksman signals an infringement.
3. An athlete overbalances in the 'Set' position.
4. Unsteadiness in the 'Set' position.

Fig 9   A 400m start showing the Starter's position to the rear of the athletes and just outside the track in the home straight.

5.   The athletes have been held too long in the 'Set' position.

6.   An athlete breaks in an echelon start where the other runners will not be aware that this has happened.

7.   An interruption such as a burst of applause, an aeroplane flying overhead or, most commonly of all, an ill-timed public address announcement.

8.   Loss of concentration by the Starter or an athlete.

FALSE STARTS

The Rules define a false start as:

'If a competitor leaves his mark with hand or foot after having adopted his final starting position and before the pistol is fired, then it shall be considered a false start.'

If an athlete false starts without the gun being fired this is called a *break*. If the gun has been fired but the athlete is judged to have anticipated it, then the terms *flier* or *beating the pistol* are often used.

It should be noted that the Rules require that races are:

'started by the report of a pistol and . . . a start shall only be made *to the actual report*.'

Study this point carefully. It means that a false start has been committed if the athlete begins to leave his mark at the moment that the gun is fired, because clearly there has not been enough time for the sound to have travelled and for the athlete to have heard and responded 'to the actual report'. Numerous physiological experiments have confirmed that there is an absolute minimum reaction time of a tenth of a second to the stimulus of the gun report. For this reason, when one runner immediately has an advantage of a metre or so on his rivals at the start, it invariably means he has had a flier or anticipated the gun, even if at the moment of the report the athlete in question was still.

All false starts must be recalled and the Rules require that the athlete responsible be warned. A second offence by the same

Fig 10 *The perfect illustration to show that it takes time for the sound of the gun to travel and for the athletes to react to the report. The gun has just been fired, as can be seen from the cloud of smoke, but all the athletes still have their hands in contact with the ground and their feet on the blocks.*

athlete in the same race carries the penalty of disqualification, except in Handicaps or Combined Events. In the former the handicap is increased for the first and second offences with disqualification for a third offence; and in the latter a second warning is given with disqualification on the third offence.

The Starter has to decide who is responsible for the false start, but he may warn two or more athletes if he thinks that more than one have caused the false start. Note that it is the athlete who is *responsible* for the false start who is warned: it may therefore be someone who does not leave the starting line himself, but who has triggered-off rival competitors by, for example, suddenly dropping a shoulder. Care should be taken not to warn athletes if the false start has been caused by some outside factor such as a camera click. The Marksmen can be very helpful in advising on this point as they are always nearer to the athletes than the Starter and are therefore better placed to judge if a false start has resulted from a disturbance among the spectators.

If a warning is imposed in a fair but decisive way there will usually be little further trouble and the race will probably get away at the second attempt. As noted in Chapter 3, the warning should be issued and recorded by the Marksmen. The Starter should instruct a Marksman to warn the offender by announcing clearly, so that all the athletes can hear: 'Please warn number . . . '

Frequent recalling is usually the sign of poor technique. A good Starter can usually detect faults so that either the athlete breaks without the gun being fired or all the competitors are told to stand up but, if it is necessary to fire a recall, the second shot should be fired after a very brief but deliberate pause. It is not good practice to fire too rapidly, because the athletes will often fail to appreciate that two shots have been fired and then a third will be necessary by which time the runners will be well down the track. The Starter should fire the recall gun after the athletes have completed their second stride and so ensure two distinct reports. While the athletes are walking back the Starter should check both his guns to ensure that the cylinders are free. A cartridge wad can occasionally cause a jam if it wedges between the barrel and the cylinder.

There are also occasions when it is necessary to recall because the start is unfair. Both Starter and Start Recaller have a duty to ensure that every athlete has a fair start. If, for example, a starting block collapses causing an athlete to stumble or perhaps impede another runner, the race should be recalled although no warning will be required. The Starter must make clear to the athletes in these circumstances that no warning is being issued, instructing the Chief Marksman by announcing, for example: 'No warning. Collapsed block in lane . . .'

After a recall or a break, for whatever cause, the athletes should be reassembled by the Marksmen. The Starter must then go through the starting procedure once more, remaining calm and, above all, not shortening his holding time.

Finally, it must be noted that the rules not only define a false start and the appropriate penalties, but also prescribe three other offences which are treated as false starts and carry the same penalty:

1. *Competitors must 'at once and without reasonable delay assume their full and final "Set" position'.* This rule is to stop gamesmanship in the form of an athlete delaying or trying to move so slowly that he either keeps his rivals waiting over-long in the 'Set', or moves so slowly that his movement is imperceptible to the Starter. It can secure an unfair advantage for the perpetrator, because he will still be moving forward when the gun is fired, and should be treated severely with a warning.

In races above 400m the requirement is that athletes adopt their final starting position after the command 'On your marks' and unreasonable delay here likewise carries a false start warning.

2. *If a competitor after the command 'On your marks' disturbs the other runners by 'sound or otherwise'.* This, again, is a rule to deal with gamesmanship and can be rigorously enforced with the aid of the Marksmen who are usually best placed to detect this form of trouble which, fortunately, is rare.

3. *A competitor must, within a reasonable time, comply with the instructions of the Marksman to come to the Assembly Line.* This rule is designed to stop athletes trying to upset their rivals by, for example, taking a long time to remove their track suits, leaving the other runners waiting stripped-off, perhaps in cold

or wet conditions.

An athlete must be disqualified if guilty of any two false start offences, by whatever combination, from the above three technical infringements and the conventional false starts of breaking and beating the pistol.

Fig 11   A break in a 100m sprint. The athlete in lane 3 has left his mark without the gun being fired. Note that the hands of the athletes on either side of him are also leaving the track. They have been triggered off by the break. Only the athlete in lane 3 was warned for false starting.

START RECALLERS

The system of using Start Recallers was first introduced by the IAAF. If a Starter overlooks a false start, for whatever reason, it allows another member of the starting team to recall the race. The team of Starters appointed for a meeting undertake the Recaller duties in turn, in accordance with a duty sheet prepared by the Chief Starter.

Start Recallers are not normally appointed below the level of Area Meetings. The reason for this is that the inexperienced Starter needs to become accustomed to taking decisions on his own, without being able to rely on another, perhaps more experienced, official to retrieve the marginal flier or to help to resolve some other problem. Self-confidence is an essential quality of a Starter and it is best developed by exposing novice Starters to the maximum amount of responsibility.

It is sensible, however, to allow Starters to practise the Recaller function before they are called upon to perform at Area Meetings. Occasionally, therefore, Recallers should be appointed at relatively minor meetings so that they can gain experience. If, for example, there are two or three Starters available, there is no harm in taking the opportunity to share duties so that some recalling practice is obtained.

Normally one Start Recaller is appointed for straight line sprint starts. He should stand just to the left or right of the Starter (beware of the recall gun!), thereby obtaining a similar narrow angle of vision. For echelon sprint races two Start Recallers are needed. They should work on or inside the track, positioning themselves to line up the athletes they are watching within a narrow angle of vision, and should always be nearer to the Starter and his gun than the athletes whom they are watching. This last point is important because it ensures that they will not hear the sound of the gun after the athletes which can make detecting a flier more difficult.

For 800m races, even with an echelon start, one Start Recaller is adequate. It is not necessary to appoint a Start Recaller for races above that distance.

The Start Recaller should always give the Starter the opportunity to recall first. If the Starter has not fired a second shot by the time the runners are about five metres down the track, the Start Recaller should fire immediately if he believes a false start has occurred. In order to give the Starter the opportunity to make the recall, Start Recallers should not cock their guns and should place their trigger finger outside the trigger guard or around the butt. This causes delay while the finger is moved inside the guard in order to reach the trigger, preventing too quick a response by the Start Recaller and so helping to eliminate unnecessary double recalls.

It must be emphasised that whenever a Start Recaller has fired the recall, the Starter is the one who decides on any warning. The Start Recaller should tell the Starter whom he adjudges to be the offender in a straight line start, but in an echelon race it is often easier if he indicates the offender by standing in the appropriate lane. The Starter then has to decide whether to accept the judgement of his colleague and issue a warning, or to stand by his own assessment. Needless to say, this must be done without acrimony between the two officials concerned.

Start Recallers should remove their caps while performing their duties. This greatly assists the Timekeepers in identifying which of the Starters will be responsible for starting the race.

CRITICISM OF PERFORMANCE

Starters and Marksmen should always avoid making any public or harsh criticism of team members during a meeting. This is unlikely to lead to immediate improvement on the day and much more likely to lead to loss of confidence and an even poorer performance. As far as possible, comments on faults should be made only at the end of the meeting and, like any observations found necessary during the competition, should always be given privately and couched in a constructive way. Affability is important. When an official performs well, and particularly if he is new to his grade, his efforts should be commended.

At this point the booklet has covered the Combined Officials' Examination syllabus. The remaining sections, as noted in the Preface, are included for general interest.

7

Indoor Athletics

The AAA and WAAA *Rules of Competition Handbooks* contain a brief appendix on indoor athletics. Race distances are, of course, affected by the size of the arena and tracks are rarely larger than a 200m circuit.

European Championships were first held some twenty years ago, and in 1987 the first World Indoor Championships were introduced. In this country there has been a steady growth in indoor competition with most of the important events being held at RAF Cosford, including national championships and international matches.

Starting at indoor meetings is no different in terms of basic principles from starting at outdoor meetings, but attention must be paid to a number of changed factors.

Firstly, as noted, tracks are smaller, usually a 200m circuit, and sprint races on the straight are only 50m or 60m. This makes the importance to the athletes of getting away well even greater than it is in a 100m race, adding to the competitive element at the start.

Secondly, a .455 inch calibre revolver has much too loud a report for a confined space and Starters should use a .38 inch, .32 inch or even a .22 inch revolver, any of which is perfectly satisfactory. In view of the reduced distance to the Timekeepers and the darker background indoors, the flash and smoke from these calibres of revolver are adequate provided that black powder cartridges are used. Proprietary starting pistols with strip magazines are not considered suitable for race, as opposed to training starts.

Thirdly, the reduced arena puts the field events in closer proximity to the track, with the result that there is much more hustle and background noise to which sprinters and Starters must accustom themselves.

Fourthly, it is rarely possible for a Starter to take up a position at the suggested 20m to 25m away from the nearest athlete. It

*Fig 12   A good start to an indoor 60m sprint. Note the
cramped conditions in comparison to outdoors. The long
jump pit and the TV cameramen are between the Starter and
the athletes, and the pole vault pit occupies much of the
foreground. The Block Recaller and one Marksman can be
seen behind the athletes (the official at the top of the banking
is a Track Umpire), but the Chief Marksman, second Marksman and the Recaller are out of picture in the right foreground.*

follows that it is extremely difficult to get an absolutely even
view of all the competitors in a 60m race, although the maximum
number of runners is usually six rather than eight. Great concentration is needed to overcome this shortcoming. Similarly,
the Start Recallers often have to adopt unorthodox positions to
carry out their duties because of the lack of space.

Marksmen have to undertake one important additional duty.
In 400m races, only the first two bends are run in lanes and the
breaking point, at the beginning of the home straight, is marked
by a coloured line. Athletes should be reminded of this when
they are assembled.

There is no reason at all to doubt that officials can benefit

Fig 13   Another view of an indoor 60m sprint. The Recaller is in the foreground, the Chief Marksman level with the starting line opposite the Starter, two Marksmen behind the athletes, and the Block Recaller on the far banking.

considerably from officiating at indoor meetings. From experience, it would seem that a Starter capable of handling a top class sprint field indoors will have no difficulty in doing likewise outdoors. The standard of starting at indoor meetings is as high as at outdoor ones, and the days have long since gone when indoor meetings were regarded as poor training for officials.

8
Major Championships and International Meetings

Officials invited to assist at major championships and international meetings will find that they need to modify their normal procedures in a number of ways.

BRIEFING

The Chief Starter and Chief Marksman will be invited to a Technical Briefing Meeting which is held well before the start of the first event in order that the Meeting Director can brief the leaders of the various disciplines. This meeting is important and officials must attend at the required time.

ADDITIONAL PRE-MEETING PREPARATIONS

Other members of the team should arrive at least one hour before the start of the meeting (not one hour before the first track event) so that they can undertake the checks outlined in Chapter 2 without interfering with the field events if, as commonly happens, one of the long throwing events is held early.

In addition, the Starters need to assist their Chief in checking the automatic timing and photo finish plug-in points for the gun. It is vital that each Starter is familiar with their location at the various start positions and has established that he is able to attach the transducer, which is connected to these points by means of a multi-core cable, to his gun with minimum fuss. The transducer is the device which activates the photo finish apparatus in response to the explosion when the gun is fired. It is important to ensure that, like the Starter's microphone, it has a sufficient length of cable attached to it to enable the Starter to take up whatever location he chooses at the start of each race.

ADDITIONAL STEWARDING AND THE MARKSMEN

Marksmen should find that their work is greatly assisted by Competitors' or Assembly Stewards. These officials will carry out clothing, shoe and number checks, as well as advising the athletes of their stations and the composition of any heats before the athletes come into the arena. Nevertheless, the Marksmen are responsible for double-checking these points, but are much less likely to encounter errors than at inter-club meetings. The preliminary check helps to make sure that any arguments or disagreements over these matters are resolved away from the start and well before the competitors come under Starter's orders.

It is customary for the Marksmen to issue photo finish self-adhesive leg numbers when checking athletes. They must ensure that the numbers are firmly affixed to the seam of the right leg of the shorts, assuming that the camera is outside the track in the normal position at the finish.

Liaison with the photo finish team is also important in case of technical difficulties, for example failure of the light on the transducer which, when illuminated, indicates that the photo finish equipment is ready for the next race. Either one of the Marksmen should be deputed to carry a radio-telephone, or a member of the Photo Finish Team should be provided with this equipment and sent to join the starting team in the field.

At most major meetings clothing baskets are provided for competitors' outerwear at the start. They are taken to the finish by teams of Clothing Stewards, normally young athletes. This helps to keep the starting area clear of personal kit and clothing. However, the Chief Marksman must make sure that the Stewards and their Leader have been well drilled so that they do not interfere with the starting procedure.

The Starters will not normally have to worry in detail about any of the preliminaries, because these matters will be in the hands of experienced senior officials, but will be able to concentrate on starting duties. It is necessary, however, for the Chief Starter to be aware of how well the preliminaries are being conducted, because it remains his overall responsibility in the event of any serious delay or disruption to try to keep the meeting to time, and he should not hesitate to intervene if a major difficulty is apparent.

TIMETABLE

Race schedules are often agreed in advance with television companies who insist that most of their transmissions should be live. Co-operation with the TV Liaison Officer in the field is essential, and fine adjustment of a minute or so either way is often needed to dovetail races, and especially feature events, into outside broadcast programmes in accordance with the pre-arranged schedules. Needless to say, this must be done with the full knowledge and agreement of the Meeting Director and without keeping athletes waiting around once stripped-off for their event.

START RECALLING

All meetings at this level will involve at least three Starters so that the Recaller system can be operated in the way previously described.

In sprint races on the straight it is now customary to appoint a Block Recaller. It is often difficult for either the Starter or Start Recaller to detect block failure promptly in a short sprint, because they are watching the runners leaving the starting line and therefore have to look back to detect that a block has slipped. The Block Recaller should position himself inside the track at the side and to the rear of the start line. His only responsibility is to watch the starting blocks and fire a recall if a block collapses or slips, thereby causing an unfair or faulty start which is not detected by the Starter (*see* Fig 2).

In recent years, at the highest levels of competition, automatic systems have been used which incorporate not only electric timing but also false start detection. These are based on pressure pads, usually fixed to the starting blocks, which indicate to the Starter by light or buzzer, and some with a time print-out, that an athlete had begun to leave the mark before hearing the gun. This is a useful aid against the sprinter who tries to get a flier, but until officials can have regular opportunity to familiarise themselves with the equipment, there is little chance that it will be used more frequently than hitherto, namely at events such as the Olympic Games.

Fig 14   The console of this false start detection apparatus is being informally tested.

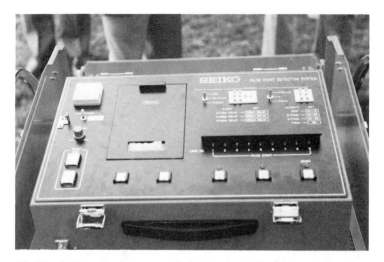

Fig 15   A close-up of the controls of a false start detection system, showing the illuminated panel and the time print-out which indicate the lane in which a false start occurs.

At this point it is worth noting that the Rules of Competition refer to races being started by the report of a gun or by 'any similar apparatus'. For years only firearms have been used, but recently some attempts have been made to develop a device which will not only convey the Starter's commands to the competitors by a conventional microphone and amplifying system but will also give a start signal, by means of a set of small electric horns, one for each runner, and, at the same time, a powerful electronic flash at the Starter's position as a signal to the Timekeepers. This would have the advantage of eliminating lethal weapons and would also ensure fairer starts when the runners are in echelon because the signal would be heard simultaneously in each lane without the time-lag of about two-tenths of a second which occurs between a pistol being fired and the sound travelling to the runner in the outside lane of a 400m race. However, it may be some time before these devices become more readily available at a competitive price, and until this is achieved traditional methods of starting and recalling will no doubt continue. When any of these systems is in use, the presence of a competent technician is essential in order to deal with any malfunctions in the equipment.

RULES

It is now commonplace for some national championships and major promotions, as well as international matches, to be held under IAAF and not national rules. This is an important point to note because there are often minor variations between sets of rules. For example, at the time of writing, national rules require an athlete to wear his number 'as issued, i.e. not mutilated or folded in any way'. IAAF rules contain no such provision. Another example relates to starting blocks: the use of blocks is optional under AAA and WAAA rules, but is obligatory up to and including 400m under IAAF rules. It is essential that these variations are carefully noted in order that the correct rule is enforced.

ALLOCATION OF DUTIES

The Chief Starter at a major promotion must take responsibility for some important preparatory work for the members of his team. Each of the Starters should be given a written set of duties before the meeting, in similar form to that shown in Appendix III, and must also be made fully aware of any special requirements arising from the Technical Briefing. It is also necessary to advise the Chief Marksman of any special requirements, to give him a copy of the duty sheet, and to ensure that he, too, has issued a written sheet to the other Marksmen (*see* Appendix IV).

It is recommended that the Chief Starter for the meeting takes responsibility for the first sprint event to try to ensure that the right standard is established at the outset. This is particularly important if he has in his team an official who is at his first major event and who may therefore be a little nervous. The less experienced official should not be given the more difficult sprint races, such as the 100m and 110mH, nor a 4 × 400m relay if the first 500m is to be run in lanes, but should be introduced gradually to the pressures of officiating at top level sprint competition, commencing with 400m races. Similarly, the Chief Starter should not allocate any of the difficult sprint races to one of his colleagues if he has reason to believe that this colleague is mildly indisposed or off-form for any reason. The allocation of duties at the highest level of competition is no place for sentiment or a 'fair shares for all' policy.

9
Conclusion

It should always be remembered that at whatever level a Starter is officiating, he is there to help the athletes by ensuring that they all get as fair and even a start as possible.

The Marksmen have an important part to play in this process by conducting smoothly and efficiently all the detailed preparations which lead up to the starting procedure, so that the athletes arrive at the start with the minimum of fuss and in the right frame of mind to perform to the best of their ability.

I hope that this booklet will help officials to achieve these aims. It only remains for me to wish the reader every success and much enjoyment from officiating at athletics meetings.

Appendix I

AN OUTLINE SPECIFICATION FOR A STARTER'S AMPLIFICATION SYSTEM

The importance of an amplification system for Starters will be apparent from the text. Many Starters like to provide their own portable system because so many tracks lack this piece of equipment. The following specification, prepared by Alan Tomkins, is intended to act as a guide to the Starter who has the practical ability to assemble a system from the standard parts that can be obtained from a good electronics kit supplier. Bear in mind when selecting the parts which make up the equipment that the finished product must be robust, in order to withstand constant handling, and must be weatherproof.

1. *Amplifier* This should be a 5 to 10 watt transistor or integrated circuit amplifier. It should operate from a 12 volt supply. Impedance matching is important so that the input matches the selected microphone and the output matches the three or four loudspeakers which must be connected in parallel. For suitable loudspeakers of nominal 8 ohms impedance, 2 to 3 ohms output will be needed.

The lower frequency response of the amplifier should be drastically reduced to ensure clarity of speech.

The gain control must be readily accessible so that the feedback can be eliminated by on the spot adjustment. More sophisticated systems can use voice-operated gain control and combined loudspeaker/amplifier units as the designer wishes. Reliability must, however, be 'built-in'.

2. *Batteries* Dry batteries are recommended for ease of transportation. Rechargeable units cost more initially and can only be justified if the equipment is in regular use. It is probably simpler to rely on HP 991 or HP 992 batteries in series, remembering always to have spares available.

3. *Microphone* Again, for reasons of portability, a microphone on a stand is not very convenient. A headphone-

microphone combination unit or a tie-clip unit is to be preferred, and must be fitted with an on-off switch.

As noted above, its impedance must match that of the amplifier input, and it should be possible to fit it with a thin plastic bag cover to keep out rain without loss of clarity and volume.

4. *Leads* The microphone to amplifier connection should be about 20m long and be screened cable of good quality. Cable from the amplifier to the loudspeakers should have strong waterproof connections, well able to withstand the inevitable mechanical stress. Simple cable reels minimise tangles and facilitate speedy setting-up of the equipment. As much as 100m of cable may be needed to reach lane 8 of a 4 $\times$ 400m echelon.

5. *Loudspeakers* Three or four plastic horn types (car roof models) are adequate. They should be rainproof and have an impedance of about 8 ohms each minimum. It is best to mount them on baseboards, partly to protect them and partly to make it easier to place them in position.

Cases for storage and carrying the equipment are advisable. This applies particularly to the amplifier, for which a storm-proof unit that can be used for protection during the meeting is essential. The cable connections as well as the other controls should be similarly protected.

Appendix II

AXONOMETRIC SKETCH OF A DESIGN FOR A STARTER'S ROSTRUM

Notes

Not to scale.

(a) Tray projects in front of the Rostrum. It should be slightly tilted towards the Starter and have two small drain holes in the corners, not more than 5mm in diameter.

(b) The wheels should be rubber tyred, 150mm in diameter and mounted on the front face so that they are 25mm clear of the ground when the Rostrum is upright. When the Rostrum is tipped forward the wheels will touch the ground.

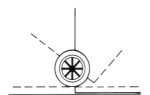

(c) Rostrum should be made of stout timber or metal construction with non-slip surfaces. The side rails and tray framework should be in 25mm tubular or square section steel with galvanised and painted finish.

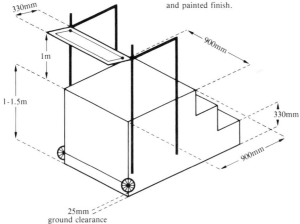

330mm

1m

1-1.5m

900mm

330mm

900mm

25mm ground clearance

Appendix III (a)

A TYPICAL DUTY SHEET PREPARED
BY THE CHIEF STARTER FOR A CHAMPIONSHIP

MERCIA AREA CHAMPIONSHIPS — Blanktown, 23–24 June
Duty Sheet for the Starters

FIRST DAY					Starter	Recall: Straight & Echelon 1–4	Recall: Blocks on Straight & Echelon 5–8
1300 hrs	3000m	Walk	Men	FINAL	GHJ	—	—
1320 hrs	100m		Men	Heats	ABC	DEF	GHJ
1340 hrs	100m		Women	Heats	DEF	ABC	GHJ
1400 hrs	400m	H	Men	Heats	ABC	DEF	GHJ
1410 hrs	400m	H	Women	Heats	GHJ	DEF	ABC
1420 hrs	1500m		Men	Heats	ABC	—	—
1435 hrs	1500m		Women	Heats	GHJ	—	—
1450 hrs	110m	H	Men	Heats	DEF	ABC	GHJ
1505 hrs	3000m		Women	FINAL	ABC	—	—
1520 hrs	100m	H	Women	Heats	GHJ	DEF	ABC
1540 hrs	100m		Men	Semi-finals	ABC	DEF	GHJ
1550 hrs	100m		Women	Semi-finals	DEF	ABC	GHJ
1600 hrs	400m		Men	Heats	DEF	GHJ	ABC
1615 hrs	400m		Women	Heats	ABC	GHJ	DEF
1630 hrs	800m		Men	Heats	GHJ	ABC	—
1645 hrs	800m		Women	Heats	DEF	GHJ	—
1700 hrs	100m		Men	FINAL	ABC	DEF	GHJ
1710 hrs	100m		Women	FINAL	DEF	ABC	GHJ
1720 hrs	5000m		Men	FINAL	DEF	—	—

SECOND DAY					Starter	Recall: Straight & Echelon 1–4	Recall: Blocks on Straight & Echelon 5–8
1400 hrs	400m	H	Men	FINAL	ABC	DEF	GHJ
1410 hrs	400m	H	Women	FINAL	GHJ	DEF	ABC
1420 hrs	3000m	St	Men	FINAL	DEF	—	—
1435 hrs	200m		Men	Heats	GHJ	DEF	ABC
1455 hrs	200m		Women	Heats	ABC	DEF	GHJ
1510 hrs	400m		Men	FINAL	DEF	GHJ	ABC
1520 hrs	400m		Women	FINAL	ABC	GHJ	DEF
1530 hrs	800m		Men	FINAL	GHJ	ABC	—
1540 hrs	800m		Women	FINAL	DEF	GHJ	—
1550 hrs	110m	H	Men	FINAL	DEF	ABC	GHJ
1600 hrs	3000m		Junior Men	FINAL	ABC	—	—
1620 hrs	100m	H	Women	FINAL	GHJ	DEF	ABC
1630 hrs	1500m		Men	FINAL	ABC	—	—
1640 hrs	1500m		Women	FINAL	GHJ	—	—
1650 hrs	200m		Men	FINAL	GHJ	DEF	ABC
1700 hrs	200m		Women	FINAL	ABC	DEF	GHJ
1710 hrs	4 × 100m		Youths	FINAL	DEF	ABC	GHJ
1720 hrs	4 × 100m		Junior Men	FINAL	GHJ	ABC	DEF
1730 hrs	4 × 100m		Junior Women	FINAL	DEF	ABC	GHJ

Notes

It is advisable to ring or colour the duty allocated to each official on his sheet. This greatly facilitates quick checking by the individual throughout the programme on the task allocated for each event.

It is impossible to divide the events absolutely evenly in terms of number of starts and distances, but this sheet strikes a reasonable balance with the Chief Starter ABC and Starter DEF, who are more experienced, taking more of the sprint events than GHJ, who is not quite so experienced. The allocation above must not, however, be regarded as definitive for any meeting with this number of events and three Starters. The experience of the Starters and the nature of the programme will vary from meeting to meeting and it is the responsibility of the Chief at each meeting to make the allocation of duties in the light of these and any other factors.

As stated earlier, it will be seen that the same Starter does the heats and finals of an event; that only one Recaller is used for the 800m and none for the longer distance events; and that the first sprint race each day is taken by the Chief Starter in an effort to establish the required standard at the outset.

Appendix III (b)

AN ALTERNATIVE DUTY SHEET PREPARED
BY THE CHIEF STARTER FOR A CUP FIXTURE

GRE Cup — Blanktown, 30 June Duty Sheet for the Starters				
		J. Brown	**W. Smith**	**T. Atkins**
12.20	10000 M	Starter	—	—
1.10	400 Hur M	Starter	R 1–4	R 5–8
1.20	400 Hur W	R 1–4	Starter	R 5–8
1.30	100 W	Starter	R Blocks	Recall
1.35	100 M	Recall	R Blocks	Starter
1.45	800 W	—	Starter	Recall
1.50	800 M	Starter	Recall	—
2.00	110 Hur M	Recall	Starter	R Blocks
2.05	3000 W	—	—	Starter
2.20	100 Hur W	Recall	Starter	R Blocks
2.30	3000 St M	—	—	Starter
2.45	400 W	Starter	R 1–4	R 5–8
2.50	400 M	R 5–8	R 1–4	Starter
3.00	1500 W	Starter	—	—
3.10	1500 M	—	Starter	—
3.20	200 W	R 1–4	R 5–8	Starter
3.25	200 M	Starter	R 5–8	R 1–4
3.35	5000 M	—	Starter	—
3.55	4 × 100 W	R 1–4	R 5–8	Starter
4.05	4 × 100 M	Starter	R 5–8	R 1–4
4.20	4 × 400 W	R 1–4	Starter	R 5–8
4.30	4 × 400 M	R 1–4	R 5–8	Starter

Appendix IV (a)

A TYPICAL DUTY SHEET PREPARED
BY THE CHIEF MARKSMAN FOR A CHAMPIONSHIP

MERCIA AREA CHAMPIONSHIPS — Blanktown, 23–24 June
Duty Sheet for the Marksmen

FIRST DAY

					Chief Marksman RST	Marksman UVW	Marksman XYZ
1300 hrs	3000m	Walk	Men	FINAL	Line on	Inside at	Outside at
1320 hrs	100m		Men	Heats	straight	rear for	rear for
1340 hrs	100m		Women	Heats	starts	straight	straight
1400 hrs	400m	H	Men	Heats		starts	starts
1410 hrs	400m	H	Women	Heats	Lanes 7 & 8		
1420 hrs	1500m		Men	Heats	on	Lanes 1–3	Lanes 4–6
1435 hrs	1500m		Women	Heats	echelon	on	on
1450 hrs	110m	H	Men	Heats	starts	echelon	echelon
1505 hrs	3000m		Women	FINAL		starts	starts
1520 hrs	100m	H	Women	Heats	Advise		
1540 hrs	100m		Men	Semi-finals	Starter	Call-up	Check
1550 hrs	100m		Women	Semi-Finals	that the	and	athletes'
1600 hrs	400m		Men	Heats	athletes	Strip-off	clothing,
1615 hrs	400m		Women	Heats	are ready		shoes and
1630 hrs	800m		Men	Heats	before	Draw if	numbers
1645 hrs	800m		Women	Heats	each race	heats have	
1700 hrs	100m		Men	FINAL		not been	Issue leg
1710 hrs	100m		Women	FINAL	Support	prearranged	numbers
1720 hrs	5000m		Men	FINAL	Marksman	by Seeders	
					wherever		
					problems	Tell athletes	
SECOND DAY					arise	qualifying conditions	
						for next round	
1400 hrs	400m	H	Men	FINAL			
1410 hrs	400m	H	Women	FINAL			
1420 hrs	3000m	St	Men	FINAL			
1435 hrs	200m		Men	Heats			
1455 hrs	200m		Women	Heats	**General**		
1510 hrs	400m		Men	FINAL	After 'On your marks' no further		
1520 hrs	400m		Women	FINAL	signal should be given by the		
1530 hrs	800m		Men	FINAL	Marksman unless there is an		
1540 hrs	800m		Women	FINAL	infringement.		
1550 hrs	110m	H	Men	FINAL	If a warning is issued, please note		
1600 hrs	3000m		Junior Men	FINAL	number of athlete and ensure he		
1620 hrs	100m	H	Women	FINAL	is aware that a warning has been		
1630 hrs	1500m		Men	FINAL	given.		
1640 hrs	1500m		Women	FINAL			
1650 hrs	200m		Men	FINAL			
1700 hrs	200m		Women	FINAL			
1710 hrs	4 × 100m		Youths	FINAL			
1720 hrs	4 × 100m		Junior Men	FINAL			
1730 hrs	4 × 100m		Junior Women	FINAL			

Notes

The duties of Marksmen UVW and XYZ can be reversed on the second day or at some other point so that each has an opportunity of undertaking both sets of duties at different times during the meeting.

If a fourth Marksman is available, each Marksman should watch only two athletes on echelon starts. Other duties should be redistributed so that the fourth Marksman assumes responsibility for making the draw, issuing leg numbers and advising athletes of the qualifying conditions.